Mansa Musa

Emperor of the Wealthy Mali Empire

Table of Contents

Introduction

Mansa Musa, an African ruler, widely known for his wealth and royalty, was an emperor who ruled the Mali Empire. The 14th century witnessed Mansa Musa's grandeur, lavish spending, and his famous pilgrimage to Mecca, which caused major changes in the Mali Empire and in a few regions around the world, namely Cairo in Egypt and some parts of Europe. To date, he is plausibly regarded as having been one of the richest people in the world, even when compared to the billionaires of the 21st century. It's believed that his total worth was around $400 billion, which is a lot more than any billionaire in today's world.

He is known for his praiseworthy devotion to Islam and how he inspired trade, economic growth, and culture in Timbuktu. His contribution to the spread of Islam was highly appreciated in the community due to his constant orders to build mosques and schools that taught Koranic values. He also encouraged students to enroll in Islamic universities in North Africa.

One of the most important highlights of his life was his Mecca pilgrimage. He was accompanied by tens of thousands of heralds and soldiers, dressed in expensive Persian silk, along with horses and camels that carried an enormous amount of gold. His return from Mecca is another interesting tale that traces his route along with various important stops and how he extended a helping hand to improve the economy of those communities.

The life of Mansa Musa is an exciting story that sparks bewilderment. This book covers the major aspects of his life, touching on important events and milestones such as his life before the reign, his rule over the Mali Empire, his expedition to Mecca, and how this pilgrimage led to major changes in his kingdom and other parts of the world. He also made noteworthy contributions that helped people in many ways, which will be covered in the last chapter. His stop in Egypt is another thrilling tale that you will soon read about in detail. Mansa

Musa's wealthy life and enterprises were so exhilarating that a few European cartographers added his drawings to maps and atlases in the late 14th century.

But his life's anecdotes are not only about generosity and giving. He conquered a lot of lands to extend his rule over Africa, including the city of Gao in the Songhai Empire, which was added to his precious count of acquired territories. These include Chad, Nigeria, Mauritania, Niger, Senegal, Gambia, Guinea, and Mali, as they are known today.

We'll also cover how Mansa Musa's reputation diminished after the Mali Empire started falling apart, turning him into more of a parodic figure than a kind king who wished nothing but prosperity for his kingdom and a good life for his citizens.

Many people are not aware of this great emperor and his interesting tale. It's time to catch a glimpse of his splendor and understand his effort to try and change the world.

Chapter 1:

Before the Reign

Mansa Musa was the grandson of Abu-Bakr Keita and the son of Faga Laye. Many speculate that he was born around the year 1280 CE. Mansa Abu-Bakr, who was Musa's brother, ruled the Mali Empire until the year 1312. Mansa Musa ascended the throne after he was appointed the deputy of the king, Abu-Bakr Keita II, who disappeared to discover the regions around the Atlantic Ocean. Mansa Musa became the Emperor of Mali in the year 1312, upon being declared as an heir to the king. The word 'Mansa' denoted an emperor in a ruling position, who also led the government of the empire. The Mali Empire saw significant changes during the rule of King Sundiata and Mansa Musa, both belonging to the same lineage.

The Mali Empire

The oldest trace that marks the plausible begin-ning of the Mali Empire dates back to the Neo-lithic period in West Africa's Sudan region, which was home to the Iron Age tumuli, a few villages, and megaliths. There was an abundance of fertile land due to the regular flooding of the Niger Riv-er in its surrounding areas, giving opportunities to the farmers to grow red-skinned African rice and millet. There was no shortage of food as herd-ing and fishing made for important food sources, too. Other food sources included harvesting root crops, pulses, fiber plants, oil, tubers, and fruits. The region was also rich in precious metals; gold and copper were regularly mined.

After the Mali Empire was established, sever-al fights and battles took place for control of the throne, mostly around the lands west of the Niger River. The first notable rule over Mali was estab-lished by a group called Soso. Initially owned by the Kingdom of Ghana (6th–13th century), their new kingdom offered them plenty of gold and wealth that could sustain the group for years. The

Ghana Empire, which was also the first notable conqueror of the Mali Empire, created its kingdom on the basis of its military power and the treasure collected from trade. By the end of the 12th century, the Ghana Empire started to regress, due to many reasons that included insufficient harvests and lack of food, regular occurrence of civil wars, and imposing acts by other kingdoms. It eventually declined after the king of the Soso group, Sumanguru or Sumaoro Kanté, took over the Empire.

Around 1235 CE, the Mali Empire was conquered by Sundiata Keita. All the Malinke people that thrived in Mali at the time were united by Sundiata Keita, who then became the ruler. It was located in West Africa and was considered to be one of the richest kingdoms of the time. Sundiata Keita, also known as Sunjata (r. 1230–1255 CE), formed an army with these people and ended the rule of Soso. Sundiata Keita defeated the Soso before they could take over the kingdom, and enjoyed the richness of Mali. As time passed, the Mali Empire conquered other regions in its vicinity, which included the Ghana Empire.

Sundiata believed that his reign over the Mali Empire was his inherited right and dauntlessly fought his rival, Sumanguru Kanté, the ruler of the Soso people. Sumanguru was known as the 'Sorcerer King' as he was speculated to have magical powers. He was claimed to summon eight spirits to assist him in winning the battle and taking over the throne. Sundiata Keita shot King Sumanguru on the shoulder with an arrow, depriving him of all his magic. He also won against the eight spiritual heads. He was, therefore, known as the 'Lion King.' He declared himself as the ruler of Mali and sought to make a lot of changes to his empire.

He began by naming the city of Niani as the capital of Mali, which was also his birthplace. It was surrounded by mountains and was located in the vicinity of water bodies and forests that were important sources of trade. He then divided the people on the basis of castes and occupations, which we'll discuss further in this chapter. He made people believe that he was the actual founder of Mali and called himself the guardian of the ancestors. He said that he had a spiritual connection with Mali, making him the rightful heir. In his prestigious rule of 25 years, he extended the empire and took control of faraway forests in the southwest, the countryside of Malinke territories, and important ports of Tadmekka and Walata.

All regions and kingdoms came forward to accept the allegiance and promised several contributions to Mali every year, some of which included grains like millets and rice along with useful tools like arrows. This was one of the reasons behind Mali's growing prosperity. Even though the Mali Empire conquered several regions, it allowed the local rulers to remain in charge of their respective territories, but under the supervision of an appointed governor from the Mali Empire. A few royal members were also kept hostage in the capital as a sign of trust and loyalty.

Heavy taxes were imposed on the citizens, as well as the goods that were traded within the Empire. However, all gold nuggets belonged to the monarch. Everyday objects like cotton, cloth, and salt were traded among citizens as currency, along with copper, gold dust, and gold ingots at times. Eventually, people were also allowed to use cowry shells from the Indian Ocean (and mainly in

Persia) as a currency that was specific to the trades within the regions of Western Sahara.

A general set of rules was followed during the reign of any Mansa. A group of local chiefs and wise elders accompanied the Mansa during important meetings and assemblies that were held in the palace. The Mansa made and declared all the important decisions and changes within the Empire, taking advice from the advisors most of the time. His group of advisors and leaders was comprised of the army chief, the master of the treasury or the granary, and the master of ceremonies, among many others. Slaves were expected to be loyal to their Mansa, and they weren't allowed to be present during the Mansa's meals. Other important customs included bowing to the king and being barefoot in his presence. The visitors also had to sprinkle some dust over their heads.

Important Trade Routes

Niani was the capital of Mali and Timbuktu served as a resourceful city with great potential for trade due to its prime location beside the Niger River. It also provided gateways for the main entry and exit, along with major land routes and waterways for the ships and merchants to visit and import goods. This gave immense power to Timbuktu to earn money, gather wealth, and become a trading hub.

The caravan routes (which were controlled by Berbers) across the Sahara Desert, as well as some important regions of West Africa and North Africa, formed a connection with Timbuktu. The coastal areas of these regions were an integral part of this trading route, too. This made it possible to export goods that were in high demand across certain regions of the world. The goods included everything from food to war utilities—sugar, kola nuts, weapons, military horses, textiles, ivory, glassware, spices, millets, stone beads, sorghum, and even slaves. Other important cities and regions that were a prime part of this activity included Gao, Walata, and Djenne, which were sooner or later used as trade centers for merchants and business owners.

The main materials and goods that were imported and exported through these routes were salt, gold, and ivory. Salt came from the northern regions while ivory and gold came from the south. The trade route was further extended to regions like the Songhai Empire, Walata, Ghana, and Tadmekka, eventually covering the Atlantic coastline. Basically, the entire trading route stretched from the Sahara Desert to the Middle East to Europe.

The Mali Empire could earn triple the anticipated amount because heavy taxes were imposed on the passage of goods and the prices were inflated. Also, the regions that were filled with gold, such as Ghana, Bure, and Bambuk, were under the reign of Mali. And because the European regions like Genoa and Venice in Italy and Castile in Spain were in constant need of gold to mint their coins, it was exported from Mali to Europe in huge quantities. All these reasons further enhanced the rich treasury of the Mali Empire.

The Culture and People of Mali

The Mali culture was highly represented by the Mande people that comprised numerous different tribes and cultural groups. Surprisingly, these people mostly shared the same languages and customs despite hailing from different tribes and groups. Also, the groups had people from different castes, who were divided as farmers, artisans, civil servants, fishermen, scribes, slaves, and many others. The farmers were regarded as the most important and respectable caste as they provided food to the entire community, which was followed by artisans.

The caste, occupation, and social division system was actually established by King Sundiata. He established this system to keep power and the 'ruling opportunity' within his family. So, the people were divided into occupations based on the family they were born into. You'd automatically be a warrior, a griot (storyteller), or a farmer if you were born into the respective families. The people did not have the right to choose their occupation but were forced to follow the family tradition.

At the time, Timbuktu was not only an important trading hub but also attracted scholars and people who wanted to learn. It was an important center of education and architecture, which was home to the then-popular Sankore University. The Sankore University educated a lot of noteworthy scholars, astronomers, and engineers, during and after the decline of the Mali Empire. The end of the University is commonly associated with the French colonial occupation, after which it was never rebuilt.

The main religion of the Malian people was Islam, but everyone had the choice to follow the religion and belief system that they preferred. The most common religious practice among the people was to follow common Islamic teachings, along with their local customs and traditions.

The majority of the Mansas converted to Islam, but they never forced their people to convert or follow it. The rulers and people adopted Islam partly because of the influence of Arab merchants they were exposed to during the trades. They also spread it to a lot of regions in Africa, mainly the west. The people that resided in the urban quarters of the empire were greatly influenced, and this attracted the religious people from the northern regions, which further influenced the people living in their vicinity. They were so devoted to Islam that a lot of Mansas took opportunities to make pilgrimages to Mecca and other holy sites.

The government of Mali ruled the entire empire by dividing it into provinces. These provinces were ruled by governors called ferba, who were majorly Muslim scribes. The governors would report to the Mansa, who led the entire government of Mali. Also, the court officials were responsible for major decisions, which also meant that the empire went through several impractical decisions that either led to instability or power of incompetent rulers. However, the prosperity of the Mali Empire can be highly credited to the ruling government bodies that took care of the administration and functioning in general. This is why the empire kept its riches and expanded despite the reign of several bad rulers. Due to all these reasons, the Mali Empire was proclaimed to be one of the richest and most powerful kingdoms in the world, so much so that it also affected the rule in Arabia and Europe.

The caste and occupation division were obediently followed throughout the reign of Sundiata Keita. However, it later fell into the hands of an ex-slave called Sakura, who ruled the region for a while. The throne was then taken over by Mansa Kankan Musa, who was speculated to be the grand-nephew of Sundiata Keita or the grandson of Abu-Bakr. Read on to understand how the rule was passed on from King Sundiata to Mansa Musa.

Lineage of Rulers

There is a lot of speculation and confusion around the bloodline of certain Mansas and their relationship with each other. The Mali Empire was powerful and expansive, but at times, it still did not have proper or sufficient leadership. Masa Wali, who was King Sundiata's son, took over the throne after his father's rule ended. The leadership was passed to his brother Wati, then to Wati's brother Kahlifa. Kahlifa was known for being a cruel ruler who killed people just for fun and entertainment. Later, the throne was passed to Abu-Bakr, who was actually Sundiata's grandchild but was adopted by him as a son. The incompetent leadership of Kahlifa and the justification of the bloodline were strong reasons behind Abu-Bakr's taking over the reign.

Sakura, who was claimed to be a military commander by some and a slave by others, overtook Abu-Bakr's rule. He later converted to Islam and made a pilgrimage to Mecca. He chose an uncommon route while traveling back to Mali from Mecca, which was through the city of Tadjoura, and he was killed midway by the Afar. People simply assumed that he was killed for the gold that he carried with him on his journey. The reign of Sakura was, however, considered to be a significant example that shows the importance and power of the court officials, which could be greater than that of the ruling family or any Mansa.

Along with the governors and mayors in every province of the empire, the trade routes and smaller regions within the Mali Empire were safeguarded by troupes and armies to avoid conflicts and keep all functions running smoothly. This is the reason why foreign visitors felt safe while traveling across the empire, and all houses had enough food. Even though the Mali Empire witnessed the rule of a few incompetent sovereigns, this division of power between court offices and the government, in general, made the functioning and stability of Mali quite adequate. Even if the main ruler didn't perform his duties well or had issues within the royal family, the divided administrative structures took care of the regional matters, which kept the economy and trade stable. And during the time of competent rulers, the empire witnessed double the growth, further extending its territory.

The Mali Empire started to regress in the 1400s and was completely ruined around 1600 CE. There were a lot of sovereigns that came to power after Mansa Musa, most of which were incapable of ruling. A few of them were either ministers or didn't even hail from Mali. However, the rule of Mansa Musa was significant and witnessed huge changes, which is an important part of history now. Keep reading to learn about the noteworthy stories of the life of Mansa Musa and his empire.

Chapter 2:

The Reign of Mansa Musa

Mansa Musa or Mansa Kanku Musa took over the throne in 1312 CE and ruled until 1337 CE. As we know by now, he began his reign when his predecessor, Mansa Abu-Bakr II, set sail to explore the ends of the Atlantic Ocean. Mansa Musa, who was the tenth ruler of the Mali Empire, contributed greatly to the prosperity of the empire and its extension across several regions. He received immense support from his general Saran Mandian, who led an army consisting of around 100,000 men and 10,000 horses. This helped Mansa Musa to expand his territory and almost equal it to the size of the Mongol Empire during that period. His rule was also established during an era when European regions faced crises and a lack of resources due to continuous civil wars and disputes.

Mansa Musa took over nearby regions such as Gambia, lower Senegal, the borders of Western Sahara, Gao, the Bure region, and the forests that were also known as the Gold Coast. It would have been impossible for the other rulers to include these regions in their empire. Mansa Musa also followed the system of dividing his regions into provinces that were ruled by different governors (known as farbas) and mayors. The main or centralized offices for this established government were based in the capital city, Niani. The economic condition enhanced further during the rule of Mansa Musa due to the continued system of paying taxes and trading of goods. The mines of gold and other precious metals were also under the control of the Mali Empire, making it richer with each passing day. The extension of the empire across various regions—including Mauritania, Senegal, Gambia, Guinea, Burkina Faso, Mali, Niger, Nigeria, and Chad—went hand-in-hand with its growth in economy and gold collection.

Development of the Mali Empire

As he was on his way to conquer more regions, Mansa Musa earned several accolades and titles such as 'Lord of the Mines of Wangara,' 'Emir of Melle,' and 'Conqueror of Ghanata.' The Mali Empire basically witnessed its second golden era with the rule of Mansa Musa. He further developed the empire by conquering the cities of Timbuktu and Gao. He also revamped the trade routes and the trading facility by improving the trans-Saharan route and relations with North Africa. During the rule of Mansa Musa, the empire was abundant in resources like gold and salt, which were also important trading goods. He owned enormous armies and horses to help him conquer the regions, along with the significant assistance of his general named Saran Mandian.

Because of this extensive rule, the empire comprised diverse people who spoke different languages, belonged to different cultures, and practiced varied traditions. The division of the government entities within these regions helped Mansa Musa to maintain his control over the extended territories and keep them functioning smoothly. This hierarchical division held by officials and soldiers in every region helped control people with different native languages, solve disputes, and collect taxes. All these records were stored in the main government office in Niani.

Spread of Islam

Due to the constant influence of Arab merchants who visited Africa during the trades, a lot of people were prompted to convert to Islam. Two prominent Muslim scholars named Ibn Battuta and Ibn Khaldun claimed that King Sundiata was also influenced to convert. Mansa Musa was known to be a devoted follower of Islam and was proficient in Arabic. He introduced the religion to his people and inspired them to covert. Because of his influence, his territory was noted to be one of the first Islamic states in West Africa. Furthermore, his justice system was also partly influenced by Islamic law. As we know, the educational centers in Timbuktu and Gao served as an important source of Islamic learning and the spread of culture. However, people weren't forced to convert, and not everyone accepted the change. This partly led to the linking of politics with religion.

A lot of rulers, including King Sundiata and Mansa Musa, converted to Islam. Sundiata's son, Mansa

Uli (also known as Mansa Wali and Yerelenku), was the first Mansa to go on a pilgrimage to Mecca, which is one of Islam's holiest sites. He made the journey in around the 1260s or the 1270s CE, which was then continued by his succeeding rulers.

The main Islamic influence on the people was made by Mansa Musa, who also commissioned the construction of mosques such as the 'Great Mosque' (also known as Djinguereber or Jingereber) in Timbuktu. He also commissioned schools and universities that promoted Islam and incorporated the values of Koran into their syllabi. Along with religion, equal importance was given to other subjects such as geography, medicine, astronomy, and history, among many others. Construction of education centers also included the establishment of libraries that contained thousands of books, manuscripts, and data that are accessible to date.

With this enormous development in education, religion, and infrastructure, a lot of people—especially the Muslim clerics—visited Mali, which increased the influence and spread of Islam. This spread was so significant throughout the regions of Africa that the people who converted started pursuing studies to become scholars or religious leaders in places like Morocco. This led Islam to be recognized as a native religion over time, instead of a foreign religion that had an influence there. Even though the religion witnessed a huge spread, a few communities still stuck to their old beliefs and refused to get influenced by the new teachings.

Islam spread further because it was taught in the Arabic language instead of the regional or native languages. This sparked curiosity among some people who were eventually attracted to it. The teachings that were held in Mali were, however, not entirely practiced in the authentic Arabic language, but in a regional variation to keep the other religious practices within the territory intact. All the beliefs, traditions, and religions were respected in Mali.

Significant Buildings, Architecture, and Art of the Empire

An important structure that represents the history and culture of Mali is the Sankore Mosque, located in Timbuktu. It is one of the most significant symbols of culture and history of Western Africa to date that speaks of the era before the colonial period. The construction of the buildings was typically done using beaten earth or banco along with a reinforcement made of wood. Beaten earth was highly used because of the absence of stone suitable for construction, and hence the architects were forced to use earth. The wooden reinforcement could be seen through the exterior surfaces, like beams. Even with the scarcity of important materials, the buildings were constructed with multiple floors and had huge, towering minarets with surprising stability.

Warehouses were also important structures due to the enormous amount of trade that was conducted at the time. Merchants stored their goods in their warehouses and lived in the 40 residential spaces or 'apartments' that were constructed within. This baked-mud architecture was significant to Mali, and there are still a few structures that stand strong, like the mosques in Djenne and Mopti. There have also been various archaeological excavations in the then-capital city of Niani, where some stone foundations, along with some parts of the house structures, were found. It was then confirmed that since stone was scarce, the richer residents paid for stone to be brought in and constructed stone houses. Another notable architectural composition of the time was a conical roof with a structure made of rammed earth bricks, wooden beams, wooden ceilings, reefs, and flooring made of earth and sand.

Lastly, the art of the region was represented through pottery and sculpture, which were passed on from the 9th century. Brass, wood, and earth were the main materials used to produce sculptures that were sometimes held by reinforcing iron rods. The sculptures often represented warriors riding on horses, or kneeling figures. It is speculated that these were produced in centers like Djenne. Music was also an important part of the Mali culture, which was often included in the famous stories told by griots that spoke of ancient tales with important historical events. Music was played during important festivals and events, accompanied by dancing.

Chapter 3:

Pilgrimage to Mecca

Whenever you hear of Mansa Musa, his famous pilgrimage to Mecca is always mentioned. One of the most note-worthy milestones and experiences in the life of Mansa Musa was the pilgrimage he made to Mecca, which is what we'll be discussing in this chapter with every detail that we know of. This journey had a lasting impact on several regions of the world, along with the Mali Empire, and is marked as one of the 'richest' and most 'life-changing' events in history. The pilgrimage took place between the years 1324 and 1325. Since Mansa Musa was a devout Muslim, he decided to carry out his duty of Hajj to Kaaba, which is in Mecca, Saudi Arabia. It's believed that every follower of Islam should perform Hajj at least once in their lifetime, which is why Mansa Musa decided to make this pilgrimage. This journey served as an inspiration for Mansa Musa to expand his empire and offer the best life to his people.

Preparation for the Expedition

Mansa Musa prepared for the journey for years. He commanded his wife Inari Kunate, along with thousands of slaves, soldiers, merchants, officials, and camel riders, to accompany him on his expedition. The total number of people that accompanied the emperor was around 60,000, out of which 12,000 were slaves or servants, and 500 were maids. A few doctors and teachers also joined the caravan.

A lot of former rulers took a journey to the far end of the Atlantic Ocean to explore the undiscovered lands. But Mansa Musa chose to go to Arabia to honor his religious beliefs. He was thoroughly prepared to cover the long distance from Mali to Mecca, which is approximately 3,000 to 4,000 miles, alongside his servants and officials. A lot of animals were collected and prepared to be taken on the expedition. These were to be used to carry luggage, people, and serve as sources of food. Camels, goats, and cows were the main animals that were taken on this journey. They were also used to carry items such as food, clothing, and a lot of gold. Around 100 camels carried 30,000 pounds of gold or more.

The journey began from the capital city, Niani, where everyone assembled and prepared to take off. The preparations included playing royal drums and a royal procession. Around 500 slaves also carried gold, and they led the journey to the destination. Mansa Musa was carried to Mecca on a camel, and he carried the official flag of the Mali Empire with him. All his people were draped in expensive clothing—mostly brocade and Persian silk—to show the empire's grandeur and wealth. His journey followed a route along the Niger River to Mema, leading to Walata, Taghaza, and then to Taut in Central Africa. Taut was an important stop for Musa as it was a trade center that witnessed continuous visits from merchants that came from Egypt and even Majorca. It also attracted traders and merchants of all religions and beliefs, the majority of which consisted of Muslims and Jews.

Stop in Cairo, Egypt

An important event during this pilgrimage was Mansa Musa's stop in Cairo, Egypt. On his route to Mecca, he crossed the Sahara Desert along with his caravan to reach Egypt. He camped with his group near the Pyramids of Giza for around three days. It took eight months for the entire group to reach Cairo. His contribution to Cairo helped uplift the economy of the region. During his stop in Egypt, Mansa Musa met the Sultan of the region, Sultan Al-Nasir, who was thoroughly impressed with the emperor's entourage and immense wealth. He noted how the Emperor of Mali had brought with him an army of soldiers, saddled horses, thousands of bodyguards, and slaves that carried their colored flags.

However, there are a few speculations regarding the meeting between Mansa Musa and the ruler of Egypt. According to ancient historian Shihab al-Umari, one of the ruler's officials invited Mansa Musa to meet the sultan. The emperor refused the invitation and explained that he was just passing through the region and that he would like to continue his journey to Mecca. There was a lot of controversy around this subject. People claimed that Mansa Musa refused to meet the ruler as he would be obliged to kiss the ruler's hand and the ground, or his feet in some variations of the story. It is believed that Mansa Musa finally gave up and agreed to meet the sultan. As anticipated, though, he refused to kiss the Sultan's feet.

The situation grew calmer when he greeted the Sultan after bowing only to Allah. He accepted accommodation arrangements for himself and his people. Mansa Musa presented 50,000 gold dinars to the sultan as a gift during their first meeting. He was given a palace to stay in during his presence in Egypt and was treated with respect wherever he went. Not only the Mansa but his wife, Inari Kunate, was also treated with the same respect and was feared by most of the people. Ibn Fadl Allah al-Umari was a renowned official and historian who accompanied Mansa Musa during most of his stay there.

Another official of the Mamluk court called Ibn Amir Hajib observed the dedication of Mansa Musa to Islam through his way of performing prayers and his knowledge of Koran. However, he also noted that the marriage practices weren't strictly followed in the court of the Mansa. This led to a serious discussion between them wherein Ibn Amir Hajib refused the Mansa's freedom of bedding beautiful daughters of his subjects outside of marriage. He explained to the emperor that this was forbidden under Islamic beliefs and laws, and shouldn't be practiced by any Muslim. Mansa Musa questioned this law and asked if kings were exempt from this rule, to which Ibn Amir Hajib replied, "Not even to kings." Mansa Musa abided by this law and never took this liberty again.

Arab historian Al-Makrizi (1364–1442 CE) quoted in Zerbo, 59: "He was a young man with brown skin, a pleasant face, and good figure...His gifts amazed the eye with their beauty and splendor." This shows the good impression and influence Mansa Musa left on the residents of Egypt.

Mansa Musa gave out a lot of gold to the people of Cairo. The residents were thrilled and sang praises for the emperor's unparalleled generosity. However, the people of Mansa Musa were overcharged in the markets of Cairo, and the shopkeepers took unnecessary advantage of the emperor's wealth.

They raised their prices and grabbed every opportunity to take hold of the gold that the people of Mansa Musa possessed.

Whether they were government officials or poor people that crossed the street, Mansa Musa gave gold to everyone and spared no one. All this generosity made the residents of Cairo rich at the time. However, the price of gold went down in value after a while, which took a major toll on Egypt's economy. It was not until 12 years later that the country's economy finally recovered. Not only Cairo, but Mansa Musa also handed out a lot of gold and money at every stop he visited on his way. Mansa Musa and his people spent so much money that they went into debt. It affected the investments that Egyptian merchants made within the territory during future trades. They took every chance to recoup the money with goods that were borrowed by the empire during the journey.

Mecca

Mansa Musa and his company stayed in Cairo for three months, after which they took off again to reach the holy site of Mecca. It is claimed that their journey was long and filled with dangers, as crossing the desert took a toll on the group in terms of thirst, hunger, and bandit attacks. Their eventual arrival in Mecca grabbed a lot of attention and curiosity among the locals and foreign visitors. People waited in long queues to get a glimpse of his royal pilgrimage.

After they reached Mecca, Mansa Musa bought houses and land for his people to stay. He ensured that all the people who followed him and took part in his pilgrimage were safeguarded and had proper lodging to stay comfortably.

Mansa Musa and his group stayed in Mecca for a few months before deciding to return home. They followed the same route for their return, and they reached Egypt once again. There are two different perspectives regarding Mansa Musa's second visit to Egypt. Some historians claim that because of his extravagant expenses during the journey, Mansa Musa had nothing to give to the people this time, as he had run out of gold and the treasure he was carrying. As a result, he had to borrow money from the lenders in Cairo to ensure his group's safe return to Mali. Other sources state that upon seeing the effects of his gold on the economy during his first visit, on his way back, he borrowed gold from Egyptian lenders at high interest in order to rectify the market and help balance the value of gold.

Return from Mecca

A lot of significant changes occurred after Mansa Musa's legendary trip to Mecca. His empire became recognized by the rest of the world—especially North Africa, Asia, and Europe—so much so that Mansa Musa is considered to be the first person to introduce the significance of West Africa to other regions and continents around the world. The trade connections increased, and relationships with merchants and traders improved. Everyone was looking for a chance to profit from the wealthy Mali Empire. And so, a lot of merchants from Morocco and Egypt traveled to Mali with caravans. They also increased their trading frequency; a lot of envoys were sent from North Africa to establish a business relationship with Mansa Musa and the empire.

The merchants were so keen on doing business and benefiting from the ruler and the empire that they built schools and mosques as generous contributions to Mali. This was also a major reason behind the spread of Islam in that region.

On his way back, Mansa Musa decided to conquer the Gao Region, which was located in the Songhai Empire. This led to his empire, extending all the way to the south of the Sahara Desert. As we've mentioned in the previous chapters, Mansa Musa built several structures of significance, a few of which were located in the Gao Region and were constructed after his return from Mecca. He also bought a glamorous audience chamber in the capital city of Niani. The famous mosque in Timbuktu, the Djinguereber or Jingereber, was and still is an important landmark of historical significance.

The architect of this building, Ishak al-Tuedjin (d. 1346 CE), was also a famous poet that hailed from Andalusian Granada. He was called from Cairo, and the fees and projects took around 440 pounds of gold, a chunk of land beside the Niger River, and a few slaves. He was called to Mali because he possessed the knowledge of different and advanced building construction techniques that could benefit the construction of new structures, especially the ones that were tall and grand like mosques. The architect lived in Mali after completing the mosque project in 1330 CE, and never returned to Cairo thereafter. The Mali Empire began to witness a distinct architectural language and style that was depicted in pyramidal minarets, burnt brick and rammed earth structures, and flat roofs that were a typical style used in the North African architecture.

Another important construction project in Timbuktu and Niani was a madugu (local name for a royal palace) with fortification walls. This was because the Tuareg group from the southern part of Sahara attacked Timbuktu for gold and tried to raid it regularly. The fortification walls were constructed as an attempt to save the city from the Tuareg. And as we know, the construction and architecture majorly depended on local materials like rammed earth and wood, because stone was scarce in the area and was only brought in from other regions for the wealthy families. The wooden reinforcement, however, proved to be strong and would function well in beams and other construction parts. The emperor's chamber in the capital city of Niani was considered to be one of the most prominent and popular designs of the architect.

Before his journey to Mecca, Mansa Musa had already contributed a lot to the spread of Islam by building mosques, schools, and universities that taught Koranic values and teachings. His pilgrimage to Mecca inspired him even more, leading him to build more universities and summon a number of books and scholars from various locations to Mali. He also brought home around four descendants of the Prophet to bless his empire and 'purify' his land with their holy presence. All this collectively led Timbuktu to become one of the main learning centers and a prime spot for education. It was also considered to be the holiest city in Mali. People would come from all over the world to visit the city and learn more about the religious values and culture that were practiced in the region. Mansa Musa also sponsored scholars and sent them to Fez in Morocco to learn more about these values. After spending some time in Morocco, the scholars would be called back to Mali and get appointed as teachers at schools and universities to share what they had learned.

Mansa Musa also brought a lot of government bureaucrats and officials, along with Arab scholars, who could help in the development of the Mali Empire. He put a lot of effort into making Timbuktu an important educational and cultural center that also promoted Islam and competed with the proliferating Islamic centers in Spain and Central India. Contrary to King Sundiata, who wanted to build an empire that followed the Malinke values, Mansa Musa sought to spread Islam throughout his empire. Even though he encouraged his people to convert to Islam, he equally respected the decision of those who wanted to follow other religions. In fact, he also performed ceremonies related to the Malinke faith.

Influence on Other Regions of the World

The story of Mansa Musa's pilgrimage got popular in Europe, and he was keenly studied by the European cartographers. A lot of famous Italian, Spanish, and German cartographers studied the region thoroughly and went on to draw maps of Mali and depicting Mansa Musa on it for about two more centuries. The first map of Mali and the depiction of Mansa Musa appeared in the year 1339 in Italy.

Around the late 14th century, he appeared in the 1375 Catalan Atlas drawn by Spanish cartographer Abraham Cresques, which was an important study tool for navigators and explorers. This pilgrimage was also the reason why popular cartographers wanted to draw the map of Western Africa in detail for the first time. His drawings represented Mansa Musa as a typical king, sitting on a throne, wearing a crown, and holding a gold nugget in his hand. He had a golden staff in one hand and a huge golden orb in the other. It was deliberately depicted in such a manner to represent his known image to the world; a king who was gleeful and proud of his wealthy empire. Today, you can find the original version of this Catalan Atlas in the Bibliothèque Nationale de France.

These tales of importance and discovery of wealth in Western Africa led more explorers and cartographers to study the potential of Timbuktu, instead of considering it to be the land of warlike tribes and terrain that was almost impossible to live on. Since there were no major references or studies of Western Africa in the earlier centuries, it was difficult for the cartographers to place the city of Timbuktu on the map, even in the 18th century. They were unaware of the potential of this culturally rich city that was developed into a major attraction for merchants, scholars, students, and traders from various regions of Africa and the world.

Another traveler from Morocco named Leo Africanus visited the capital city of Niani after the visit to Mecca and was immensely impressed by its people. He found the residents to be quite intelligent, civilized, and highly respected among all people in the regions of Western Africa.

A renowned African Muslim scholar named Mahmud Kati made an important note in his book called "The Chronicle of the Seeker" in the year 1987, in which he mentions what could have inspired Mansa Musa to make his pilgrimage to Mecca. He says:

"The Mali-koy Kankan Musa was an upright, godly, and devout sultan... The cause of his pilgrimage was related to me as follows by the scholar

Muhammad Quma, may God have mercy on him, who had memorized the traditions of the ancients. He said that the Mali-koy Kankan Musa had killed his mother, Nana Kankan, by mistake. For this, he felt deep regret and remorse and feared retribution. In the expiation, he gave great sums of money in alms and resolved on a life-long fast. He asked one of the ulama of his time what he could do to expiate this terrible crime, and he replied, 'You should seek refuge with the Prophet of God, may God bless and save him. Flee to him, place yourself under his protection, and ask him to intercede for you with God, and God will accept his intercession.'"

Another North African scholar paid tribute to Mansa Musa's important life events and praised the power of the emperor, declaring him as "the most powerful, the richest, the most fortunate, the most feared by his enemies and the ablest to do good for those around him."

This noteworthy expedition conducted by Mansa Musa surely caused a lot of changes, not only in other regions of the world but within the Mali Empire. The empire mainly witnessed great economic

improvement, an increase in trading opportunities, advancements in the education and learning
system, and worldwide recognition. The emperor
was one of the main reasons why Mali was put on
the map and recognized for its immense power.
An important traveling exhibition called "Caravans of Gold, Fragments in Time: Art, Culture and
Exchange across Medieval Saharan Africa" always
mentions Mansa Musa and his historic pilgrimage tale, along with his influence on Cairo and his
immense wealth. Mansa Musa's pilgrimage experience is also spread throughout the world in the
present day. A lot of movies and documentaries
have been made, and books have been written on
this subject.

In the upcoming chapter, we'll discuss further
changes that were witnessed in the Mali Empire
after Mansa Musa's return from Mecca. We'll also
take a look at the state of the empire 12 years after
Musa's death, from the perspective of Ibn Battuta,
who was a renowned Moroccan traveler and writ-
er.

Chapter 4:

Through the Eyes of Ibn Battuta

A s we've mentioned in the previous chapters, the changes within the Mali Empire were exemplary after Mansa Musa's return from Mecca. He was inspired by a lot of people, mainly scholars, architects, and saints during his journey. He either brought a few of them back with him to Mali or seek advice on the type of changes that were required for the development of Mali. Timbuktu and Niani were developed into major cultural and educational centers, and people from other regions of Africa and the world visited Mali to establish business and to earn from the riches of the empire. Mali was at the peak of its prosperity in the 14th century, due to the efforts and contributions of Mansa Musa.

We know the scale at which Mansa Musa worked to make all these changes and improve the lives of his people. But what happened after a few years of making these changes? Did Mali continue to prosper in the same way? Did Timbuktu and Niani garner the same attention after a decade? Let's find out. In this chapter, we'll also see how the Mali Empire was affected after the death of Mansa Musa, through the perspective of a scholar and traveler named Ibn Battuta, and his experience of meeting the Mansa of the time.

About Ibn Battuta

Abu Abdallah Ibn Battuta was a scholar who explored various regions of Africa and Asia for around 30 years. He was born into a Muslim family in Tangier, Morocco, in the year 1304. It was a prominent family whose members included renowned judges and scholars. Learning Sharia, based on Koranic values and the teachings of the Prophet Muhammed, was considered mandatory in his family in order to become a qadi (a Muslim judge).

When the notable traveler Marco Polo died in the year 1325, Ibn Battuta set sail to travel across continents—a wide range of land covering around 75,000 miles, much higher than what Marco Polo covered. He was just 21 years old when he decided to leave home and explore the world. He began by making a pilgrimage to Mecca, which lasted around 16 months, not returning home for almost 24 to 30 years. His journey continued until he reached the east of Asia, and he visited a few places in China and India. He also explored regions in Syria, Palestine, Arabia, Persia, South Asia, Turkey, Eastern Europe, and the Mediterranean coast. He also explored Spain and numerous places in Africa.

After his return, his travel stories were mentioned in a traditional Arabic travelogue known as a rihla. It was commissioned by the local sultan and was noted by a young scholarly official. This travelogue was perceived to be a source of immense knowledge due to the mentions of real-life experiences and lessons that Ibn Battuta went through. He settled in Fez, Morocco, for the rest of his life, and continued to work there as a judge until his death in 1368 or 1369.

The travelogue and records of his journey were confined to the North African world until German explorer Ulrich Jasper Seetzen got hold of a copy in the 19th century. The tales took to the world after they were first published in a lot of French and German journals in the year 1818. His travelogue got translated into English in 1829 for the first time, after which Ibn Battuta's entire work kept being translated until 1994. You can find his complete work in four volumes today.

One of his noteworthy travel tales dates back to the time when he decided to visit Mali in 1353.

Ibn Battuta's Travel to Mali

Among the many people that traveled to and explored the Mali Empire to gain knowledge, Ibn Battuta made a small but significant contribution to it. He traveled to Mali in the year 1353 after hearing about the devout Islamic following and how the empire was molded into an Islamic learning and cultural center. A part of Dar al-Islam, the Mali Empire extended as far as the Atlantic Ocean and covered the city of Gao, the stretches of the Niger River, and many present-day countries like

Senegal, Mauritania, and Mali. He learned that the religion of Islam started to be adopted as early as 800 CE when Arab traders visited the region and certain areas of the Sahara Desert to conduct trade and earn gold. Slowly but steadily, a lot of traders adopted the religion along the borders and within the central regions, and Islam had become an official religion by the year 1200.

The story of Ibn Battuta's travel to Mali was translated into a lot of languages, mostly in the first-person point of view. This chapter will cover his journey and experience through his perspective, but not in the first person. It's important to reflect on the story of Ibn Battuta because it shows the general characteristics of the empire, the emperor, and the people left behind by Mansa Musa. His presence and rule had a lot to do with the way the Mali Empire turned out to be.

Beginning the Journey to Mali

Ibn Battuta started his journey with three friends and hired a guide from the Massufa. They estimated the journey to take around 24 days from Iwalatan and decided not to waste any time. On his way,

Ibn Battuta curiously described the trees and their physical features—their girth, age, and how they provided passers-by with shade, food, and water. He also noted that the traveler had to buy the goods and grains that were popular in Mali. The women in the villages on their main route would bring grains, milk, chicken, millet, rice, fruit, and other food items that were majorly harvested within the empire to sell it to the travelers.

The route also included regions like Kabara and Zagha along the Nile River that were conquered by the emperor. The residents of Zagha were devout Muslims that were determined to study and acquire precious knowledge. The route continued along the Nile, leading to Timbuktu and Gao, followed by the town of Muli (the town was inhabited by a group of people known as the Limis), and then to Yufi. However, no white people were allowed there, and they would be killed if they entered.

During his journey to Central Mali, Ibn Battuta went through exhilarating experiences, particularly during a few instances. Along the Nile River, he noticed a crocodile on the bank that looked similar to a boat. When he approached the bank to fulfill a need, his path was blocked by one of the locals. It was then clear that the person was protecting him from the crocodile by standing in the middle. After experiencing similar encounters with the locals, he finally made it to the capital city of Mali.

Reaching the Destination

As soon as he reached the capital, he started looking for a person named Muhammad ibn al-Faqih, who had arranged for his lodging during his visit. He received a warm welcome with food and candles and was personally visited by Ibn al-Faqih. He was also welcomed by other prominent figures within the city, such as Abd ar-Rahman, who was the qadi of Mali and Dugha, serving as the interpreter. Ibn Battuta claimed that these people were very generous, kind, and welcoming. They also gave him several gifts and offered all sorts of help. Ibn Battuta was thoroughly impressed with their gestures and wished them good luck.

After a few days, one of his acquaintances, among a total of six, died because of eating a gruel made of a root that was similar to colocasia. The others fell ill, and Ibn Battuta fainted during his morning prayer. A remedy was offered by an Egyptian resident who made baydar, a mixture of sugar, aniseed, and vegetable roots in water. He drank it and vomited the food, but still stayed sick for the next two months.

His Meeting with the Mansa

Ibn Battuta finally met the Mansa of Mali at the time, Mansa Sulayman. His personal experience led Ibn Battuta to portray the king's character as miserly and unwelcoming as he didn't receive any presents during the two months that he spent sick. A ceremony was held to commemorate Master Abu'l-Hasan, and people of prestigious positions were invited, like commanders, officials, doctors, preachers, and the qadi. The ceremony included readings from the Koran and prayers for Abu'l-Hasan and the king.

Ibn Battuta met the king, and he was asked to offer his gratitude to Allah. He also received a gift, which he was asked to receive by standing up. He expected to find money and honorable robes in it. Instead, he received fried beef, cakes of bread, and sour curd, further proving his viewpoint about the king's character.

The court ceremonies held to honor the king were similar to festivities. The ceremony was usually held on the pempi, which was a platform built under a huge tree with silk carpets and heavy cushions. The king was adorned with expensive clothing (generally a velvet tunic known as the mutanfas), and he carried a bow and a quiver in his hand and back, along with a golden skull cap on his head. His procession was accompanied by drums and music, along with numerous slaves. The deputy and military commanders were called, and two decorated horses and goats were presented to the court as signs of protection. The audience had to witness the ceremony, standing under the trees.

The people were required to respect the king and call out his name by chanting 'Mansa Sulayman ki' to show respect, as per the tradition of Mali. If the king called someone from the crowd, the person had to change his clothes, knock the ground with his elbows, and throw dust on his head and back. Apparently, the act of showering dust over one's back after receiving a remark was considered to be good manners and a polite reply to the king.

Good and Bad Qualities of the People of Mali

During his stay, Ibn Battuta encountered several incidents that showed the good and bad qualities of the people of Mali. Their best quality, according to him, was their conduct of justice. If any person was guilty of any crime, they were never spared by the king. The factor of security in the empire was also impressive. There was hardly any violence or incidents of theft. Also, confiscation of anyone's property, unless they were slaves, was off the limits. When a person died, the property or treasure would be passed on to their heir or any trustworthy person who could find a suitable heir.

Malian people were also very strict with the prayer timings. Every man had to visit the mosque and prayer hall during the early hours to find a spot to pray. Their appointed prayer boys were sent to the mosque to secure a spot and spread their praying mats for them. It was also important to wear clean clothes, especially on Fridays. However old the garment was, it had to be washed before being worn to the Friday prayers.

The bad qualities included punishing kids to learn the Koran. The people forced their children to learn the Koran by heart. If not done so, they'd go to extreme lengths and tie their kids in chains until they could recite it. Another bad quality was the disrespect of women in terms of clothing. Every woman, including the servants, daughters, and slaves, were expected to wear no clothing. They were also expected to see the king without any clothing. These people also ate animals that included donkeys, dogs, and carrion. These bad qualities left Ibn Battuta unimpressed.

Festivities in Mali

The main festivities of Mali, among many, were breaking the fast and sacrifice. The festival ceremonies were almost similar to the court ceremonies, except that the bearers brought tons of gold accessories and precious swords in the former. The rest of the seating took place as designated in the court ceremonies. The Dugha was accompanied by his wives and slaves (all women), and he played music on a reed instrument with poetry and calabashes. The show then got extravagant with the slaves and wives singing along, the youth playing drums, and young boys spinning wheels and playing with swords to entertain the king and the audience. At the end of the ceremony and the following day, the Dugha was presented with gifts by the king and people of all ranks. The most common present given by the king was gold dust.

During the festivities, when feasts were held, several poets were adorned with makeup and accessories. They recited poems that wished good deeds and good luck upon the king. They then performed an old custom that had been continued for ages and was considered important. The chief poet placed his head on the king's lap, his right shoulder, and then his left shoulder.

The Day of Departure

Ibn Battuta stayed in Mali for almost two years, and his day of departure finally came on the 22nd of Muharram, 1354. He rode a camel and was accompanied by Abu Bakr, who was a merchant. After a while, they reached a channel across the Nile River and decided to cross the path during nightfall to avoid mosquitoes that infested the area during the day. He saw a species of animals that were huge in size and piqued his curiosity. Initially thought of as elephants, they turned out to be hippopotami. These animals appeared again along the river route that led toward Timbuktu and Gao. Ibn Battuta witnessed a few people hunting hippopotami by throwing spears at them. This encounter shows that people hunted hippopotami for their meat and skin in the 14th century.

Another interesting encounter for Ibn Battuta was when he met Farba Magha, who accompanied Mansa Musa on his pilgrimage to Mecca. During this encounter, Ibn Battuta learned that Mansa Musa had a qadi who was planning to steal four thousand mithqals. When the king found out, the qadi was banished to a country inhabited by heathen cannibals. The heathens didn't eat him because they didn't consider white people to be 'ripe' enough to be eaten. So, he was sent back to his country.

Reaching Timbuktu and Gao

Ibn Battuta was eager to visit Timbuktu as he had heard about the development of the city and the caliber of the residents. He met the then-governor of Timbuktu, Farba Musa, and learned about the inhabitants and culture of the place. Ibn Battuta and his companion then left for Gao. They stayed in Gao for around a month and claimed it to be one of the best regions in terms of provision. There was no scarcity of food; rice, fish, and milk were found in abundance.

The journey of Ibn Battuta shows the commonalities and changes that the Mali Empire faced after the reign of Mansa Musa. According to his account, while the riches and grandeur still remained, the emperor of the time wasn't as generous as Mansa Musa.

Chapter 5:

Mali After Mansa Musa

Mansa Musa died in the year 1337 and left a lasting impression and influence on the world. His son, Mansa Maghan I (r. 1337–1341 CE), ascended the throne after him. He had experience in ruling the empire as regent when his father was on his way to Mecca. The throne then passed to his brother Mansa Sulayman (c. 1341–1360 CE). It is speculated that his uncle took over the reign through foul means after he ruled for around four years, but there's no evidence on the same. However, it is known that Mansa Sulayman promoted his religion to his people and all around Western Africa. The Mali Empire witnessed continuous growth, even after witnessing the rule of numerous emperors. It went on to prosper for another century until the colonization took place.

The land and neighboring regions slowly started deteriorating when new gold mines were discovered, and new trade routes were used to import and export goods through the southern coast of West Africa. By the mid-15th century CE, the trading business was diminished on a large scale. Other kings and Mansas were also involved in civil wars among themselves, and all of this eventually led to the fall of the Mali Empire. It was followed by attacks on the main cities within the empire, such as Timbuktu, by the Tuareg group. King Sunni Ali (r. 1464–1492 CE) then fought to demolish the Mali Empire and expand the Songhai Empire, which thrived in the 1460s. We'll go through these events in detail to understand the fate of the Mali Empire and how it came to be what it is in the present day.

The Mali Empire during the Mid-14th Century

As we know by now, Mansa Musa dedicated a lot of energy, power, and resources to improving the condition of the Mali Empire and making it an educational hub, along with a center of strong religious beliefs. The empire continued to make more money and witnessed further economic growth after the rule of Mansa Musa. He had made Timbuktu, Djenne, and Walata the prime commercial centers and improved the architecture of the place. Trades and business improved with more incoming merchants. Mali was being recognized outside Africa, and Mansa Musa was drawn on important maps and atlases by European cartographers.

Improvement in Infrastructure

We also know about the construction of structures like universities and mosques in Djenne and Timbuktu. It's important to mention it again because it was one of the greatest changes that influenced the growth of Mali. The Sudano-Sahelian architectural style that was introduced through these structures was noteworthy and got popular across the globe. The Great Mosque in Djenne was reconstructed in the year 1906. The project was headed by the leader of the mason guild of that region, Ismaila Traore, and it took around two to three years for it to finish.

The improvements in Timbuktu's performance can be noted through the perspective of Leo Africanus, which he mentioned in his book titled "Description of Africa" in 1550. He wrote about the inhabitants and their way of living in Timbuktu, and how it evolved over the years.

According to him, the houses were made with thatched roofs and clay-covered wattles that represented hut-like structures. The central temple and king's palace were designed by the same architect, using materials like stone and mortar. There were numerous shops operated by merchants and shopkeepers who sold various products. The Berber merchants brought cloth and fabric from Europe, and women were expected to cover their faces with veils. The majority of the residents were rich, and the king of the time agreed to wed his daughters to two rich businessmen. There was no shortage of food, water, animals, and grain. But there was a shortage of salt because it was imported from Tegaza.

Other important mentions in his excerpt included the smooth functioning of the king's court. Books, many of which were hand-written, were imported from Barbary, and literacy was widespread. The people lived harmoniously and went for walks in the evenings. Many of them even enjoyed those walks by dancing and playing music. Basically, the city of Timbuktu was claimed to be a land of fortune.

Rise and Fall of the Songhai Empire

In the mid-14th century, the Mali Empire began to regress, witnessing a major fall by the 15th century. Even though it survived in the following years, it had lost a lot of importance and power by that time. One of the main reasons for this was the rise of the Songhai Empire. As soon as the Mali Empire began to fall, the Songhai Empire took advantage of the timing and worked on the complete regression of the Mali Empire. Gao was established as the capital city of the Songhai Empire, and it started to expand further. The empire gradually acquired more power and took control of many cities. It had also taken over the city of Timbuktu by the end of the 15th century.

The Songhai Empire was taken over by the Saadi Dynasty of Morocco in 1591. They did this by fighting the Songhai in the Battle of Tondibi. Slowly but steadily, they took control over cities like Gao, Timbuktu, and Djenne, which once belonged to the Mali Empire. The Saadi Dynasty, however, couldn't control the entire empire on its own. A lot of other kingdoms fought for various regions within the empire and succeeded. These included (not in order of rule):

- The Bambara Empire mainly controlled the southern and central parts of Mali along with Segou and Timbuktu. It was defeated by a Toucouleur conqueror named El Hadj Umar Tall, who then took over Segou in 1861.

- Another Bambara state was established when the Coulibaly Dynasty was split. It gave rise to the Kingdom of Kaarta and was also taken over by Umar Tall in 1854.

- Another state that was established against the rule of Segou was the Massina Empire, which was later defeated by Umar Tall in 1862.

- Other noteworthy kingdoms included the Kenedougou Kingdom, the Toucouleur

Empire, and the Wassoulou Empire. They remained somewhat connected to the French conquerors until the end of the 19th century.

French Colonization and Independence

The French colonized Mali in the year 1892. Mali was renamed as French Sudan or Soudan Français, and a civilian governor was appointed to take control. The French took over the place entirely in 1905. Since there was no formal power or rule before colonization, the region started to regress, and the agriculture declined. The French took advantage of this and started to use the region's raw materials for their manufacturing processes. They also conquered the cities of Gao and Timbuktu in the years 1898 and 1894, respectively. The main raw materials that were produced in Africa under the French rule were peanuts and cotton. The region also saw the development of railways and roads to make transportation and export easier.

Taxes were imposed, no means of communication or education were established, and internal trade networks weren't developed, either. Mali remained under the rule of colonists for around 70 years, from 1890 to 1960. The years from 1899 to 1904 witnessed the administrative merging of Mali with Niger, Burkina Faso, Senegal, and Mauritania (present-day countries). The merging of Mali with Niger, Burkina Faso, and Mauritania was named as "Haut-Sénégal et Niger," meaning Upper Senegal and Niger. Basically, the borders weren't defined and kept on changing now and again. Bamako was the capital of the colony and was expanded between the years 1902 and 1912.

The French rulers encouraged peasant production and exploited the inhabitants. Labor was constantly supplied to other colonies in the western part of the continent.

A federation that consisted of Senegal and the Sudanese Republic gained independence on 30th June 1960. Since the two parties faced political differences, the federation separated on 20th August.

Present-Day Mali

Mali has faced a major downfall in economic and natural conditions since its independence. With continuous natural issues like periodic droughts and less rainfall, Mali has witnessed a decline in agriculture. It is also known for the governmental issues that it has faced, like ethnic unrest and heavy duties by the bureaucracy. With the onset of Marxist policies and oppressive military government rule, Mali went through a lot of social and economic tensions over the 20th century. Furthermore, the official currency faced devaluation by 50% in 1994, which caused major tensions and riots.

A lot of these reasons, combined with the Tuareg rebels and riots between Fulani herders and Soninke farmers, were enough to make Mali poor. It was on the verge of economic development by the end of the 1990s, but the trading and exports from the country decreased, and petroleum prices increased. This led Mali's per capita GNP to stay around $270 in the year 2000. It is actually considered to be one of the poorest countries in the world with a high population. Around 82% of the labor force within the country is involved in agriculture, making it their main source of income. The country's literacy and life expectancy rates are extremely low. It is somewhat ironic that what was once one of the richest regions in the world is currently facing such a challenging economic crisis.

Conclusion

Y ou now know basically everything about Mansa Musa of Mali and his life, along with his travel anecdotes and how he had an impact on his empire. Let's have a quick recap of what we have learned about the wealthiest king that ever lived.

The Mali Empire, between the years 1312 to 1337 CE, ruled by Mansa Musa, was one of the richest empires, not only in Western Africa but in the world. The Mali Empire gained immense wealth by serving as the major trading hub in Western Africa. The trading activities were focused on materials like gold, ivory, and salt. Their culture was influenced by the Arab merchants that visited the region frequently and prompted the aboriginal rulers to adopt Islam. When Mansa Musa ascended the throne of the already-flourishing Mali Empire, he made reforms in his administration by dividing his empire into provinces and appointing governors to govern them. They recorded the administrative activities, and these records were sent to the capital city of Niani, which led to the empire's further increase in wealth.

Extensive records mention and praise Mansa Musa's devotion to Islam and his generosity toward his people, as well as the inhabitants of Cairo during his pilgrimage to Mecca. His generosity blinded his needs. He gave away all the gold he had as presents and was speculated to go bankrupt himself. Upon reaching Mecca, he purchased land and arranged for lodging to accommodate the people that accompanied him on his pilgrimage. While in Arabia, he was inspired by the holy sites, the architecture, and the culture in general. He took along a lot of scholars, architects, and artisans with him from various cities back to Mali. He was so inspired that he built a breathtaking audience chamber at Niani and remarkable mosques in Gao and Timbuktu.

The most famous mosque also called "The Great Mosque" located in the city of Djenne, is marked as an architectural marvel. A famous architect,

Ishak al-Tuedjin from Cairo, designed these notable buildings. Mansa Musa's rule lasted 25 years, during which the tales of the rich Mali Empire spread far and wide. As a consequence, cities like Timbuktu were ravaged by the Songhai Empire, which led to the collapse of the Mali Empire and its colonization.

Mali is known as the Republic of Mali today, and it is still the third-largest producer of gold and salt in Africa. The irony is that the richest empire in the world, which was once worth $400 billion, has a GDP of $17.6 billion as of 2019.

The key points to be extracted from the entire tale of Mansa Musa are:

- Introduction of a different architectural style to the world

- The recognition of Western Africa in the other parts of the world

- The wealth of the Mali Empire

- The spread of Islam in the western and northern parts of Africa and the empire's influence on it

- The growth of Timbuktu and Mali in general

This tale puts Mansa Musa in a good light because of his generosity, the reforms he made in his administration, and his attitude toward people of different faiths. All in all, Mansa Musa was well-known for the immense wealth he possessed, and his legacy deserves recognition in the present day, as well.

Thank you for reading this book.

Resources

https://www.ancient.eu/Mansa_Musa_I/

https://www.ushistory.org/civ/7b.asp

https://www.ducksters.com/history/africa/empire_of_ancient_mali.php

https://www.ancient-origins.net/ancient-places-africa/mali-empire-0011696

https://www.ancient.eu/Mali_Empire/

https://www.sahistory.org.za/article/empire-mali-1230-1600

https://www.ancient.eu/Mansa_Musa_I/

https://www.thefamouspeople.com/profiles/mansa-musa-33307.php

https://www.ushistory.org/civ/7b.asp

https://www.ancient.eu/Mali_Empire/

https://amazingbibletimeline.com/blog/mansa-musas-pilgrimage-mecca/

https://www.paperwritings.com/free-examples/pilgrimage-taken-by-mansa-musa-of-mali-1324.html

https://www.history.com/news/who-was-the-richest-man-in-history-mansa-musa

https://www.ancient.eu/Mansa_Musa_I/

https://www.blackpast.org/global-african-history/musa-mansa-1280-1337/

https://aboutislam.net/family-life/culture/historic-hajj-mansa-musa-king-mali/

https://www.ancient-origins.net/history-famous-people/mansa-musa-richest-man-history-006847

http://mrsmiddlebee.weebly.com/uploads/1/3/5/0/13506833/4.3_ibn_battuta_to_mali.pdf

https://www.crf-usa.org/bill-of-rights-in-action/bria-18-1-c-ibn-battuta-the-greatest-traveler-in-the-middle-ages

https://www.ancient.eu/Mansa_Musa_I/

https://www.sahistory.org.za/article/grade-7-term-1-kingdom-mali-and-city-timbuktu-14th-century

http://www.doe.virginia.gov/instruction/history/mali/history/index.shtml

https://www.britannica.com/place/Mali/Precolonial-history

Ingram Content Group UK Ltd.
Milton Keynes UK
UKHW021829110723
424957UK00011B/688